A cup of Rainbow Dreams

Rija E Mathew

BookLeaf Publishing

India | USA | UK

Presentation by *BookLeaf Publishing*

Web: www.bookleafpub.com

E-mail: info@bookleafpub.com

ISBN: 9789360941819

First edition 2024

DEDICATION

For my son, Ninan John, Be brave, You are a Hero

ACKNOWLEDGEMENT

In this book I want to acknowledge all the hands of love and kindness that have touched me in my life, all my passing friends, all my lost friends, all the mothers and sisters, all the brothers and cousins, all the nieces and nephews. The list is endless to name all.

I extend my heartfelt appreciation to my parents, Dr John Mathai and Dr Moni Ann Thomas, my husband Mr John Ninan, my son Master Ninan John, my sister Rima and her family, my precious niece and nephews Ms Hannah, Master Varun and Master Adon for their constant support and inspiration. I am grateful to my husband's family Mr Ninan John, Mrs Anitha Ninan, Mr Kuruvilla John, Mrs Suja Kuruvilla and Mr Joseph Ninan. I take this opportunity to remember my family who has helped me several times with their love and support, including my Uncle Capt Issac, Laaly aunty, my cousins Mr Nikhil, Mr Nithin, Eldho uncle, Leena aunty, Ms Neethu and Ms Nikitha.

Special mention must be made of two amazing ladies whom I have placed deep inside my heart Mrs Sudhamani Madam and Mrs Padma Madam. Both of them took me under their wings at the workplace and showered me with their love, care, food and wonderful life lessons.

Above all, this book is made possible by the "Almighty Creator" who resides in all of us. He made the words flow through my pen and made this dream a reality. Thank you.

PREFACE

We are all living a busy life, myself included. I am so busy with my regular job, several hours of travel daily to my workplace, taking care of my son, trying to squeeze in half an hour of exercise daily and not slack off in my prayer and meditation routine, that I am left with almost no time to sleep. So I am left walking around like a zombie with no energy and no intention, just a constant running to be somewhere or complete some job at home or office. But life is strange and blessings do come in disguise. If someone had the nerve to tell me that the transfer in my job would turn out to be a blessing, I would gladly have given them a beating. Because with the transfer, my health and my life were tossed into turmoil and I hated it. But almost 1.5 years have passed and I have cracked a very, very tough exam after almost 10 years, published a poetry book and am now going to publish my second book. Thus my greatest dream since childhood, "To be a published author even if nobody reads my book," has come true, all thanks to the hours of daily travel. And glad to say, a few people have read my first book and have given glowing comments about it. So I welcome you to enjoy this book, which I have written to brighten up my life and the life of all those who read it. Have a pleasureful read.

TABLE OF CONTENTS

BE A STORY, WEAVE A STORY

Be a story, weave a story,
One that inspires and moves,
One to treasure deep inside your heart,
Like your favourite bedtime story.

Weave a story with your life,
Give it the tone, timing and set you choose,
Wave your magic wand and design your
marvellous middle,
Plan each page to fabricate the perfect ending.

Be a story, weave a story,
Filled with success and failures,
Let each regret propel forward,
To a life where fulfillment outweighs all
remorse.

Be your best story, weave your own story..

COFFEE PLEASE

When morning grogginess hits the head,
Coffee please, to unfog the thoughts.

When midday lethargy hits the limbs,
Coffee please, to charge them up.

When nostalgia haunts and hurts,
Coffee please, to ease the ache.

When cousins and friends meet up,
Coffee please, to spice up the moment.

When hunger strikes unexpectedly,
Coffee please, to satiate the pangs.

When bored and lost with no direction,
Coffee please, to soothe and snuggle.

LET ME BE THE ONE

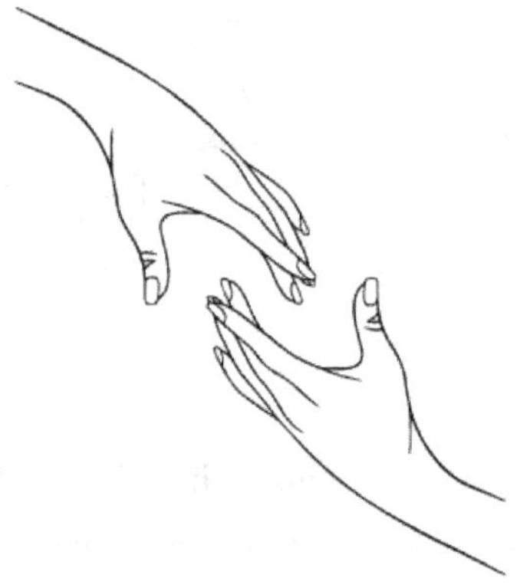

When this strange journey troubles you dear
child,
Let me be the one to calm you,
When the sensory overload disturbs your mind,
Let me be the one to comfort you,
When life throws curve balls at you incessantly,
Let me be the one to shield you,
When your fatigued limbs refuse to budge,
Let me be the one to carry you,
For dear one, you are closer than my heart and
soul,
And I love you more than life itself.

GOLDEN MEMORIES

There is a whole book of memories in my head,
Only the place exists in reality,
The loving characters have passed away,
The rest of us are scattered like chaff,
Living in different corners of the world,
Here and there, remnants of the group survive,
Although now not united under the same
umbrella as in olden days,
The bonds of love still survive,
Unhindered by the distance and continents
separating us,
Yet it is not the same,
The camaraderie of those golden days haunts
and leave a tear,
We who shared the same experiences at one
time,

The ones who shared the stories and food
prepared by the same loving hands,
No longer exists,
We have grown and evolved,
With our own families and friends and jobs,
The current experiences do not merge,
Yet we are connected by the magical threads of
the past,
Those memories will never fade,
But remain etched in time.

MOTHER

In a chaotic world,
You are my anchor,
And when your face darkens like a
thundercloud,
I feel like a ship tossed around in a hurricane,
As if my soul has lost its bearing,
So please stay sane and calm for me,
For right now you are my whole world mother,
And I love you with my whole small heart.

SAY YES TO LIFE

Say Yes, if it scares you,
Say Yes, when you think it might be beyond
you,
Say Yes, if you think you can't do it,
Say Yes, if it challenges you,
For you only truly overcome yourselves,
If you say Yes, to hardship and pain,
So never give up on your faith,
Keep moving forward,
Walk if you can't run and plod if you can't walk,
But never stop moving,
Have unshakeable faith in your vision,
And it shall be done as you believe,
Say Yes to growth, say Yes to success,
Say Yes, even when you are failing,
For failure is your ticket to success.

BETTER TODAY

Remember to smile today,
Remember that everything will pass,
Remember to be kind to family,
For only heaven knows if we will wake up
tomorrow,
Remember to share your umbrella today,
For tomorrow you may need one,
Remember to share your strength with the weak,
For the shy one may not be just an introvert,
But battling with anxiety disorders and phobias,
Remember everything is not as it seems,
Most things have a depth you cannot fathom,
Remember that there are many unseen heroes
around you,
The ones who face their fears everyday,
Unseen and unheard, they plod on bravely,
Remember to shine, for your light matters,

Remember to leave each day a little better than yesterday.

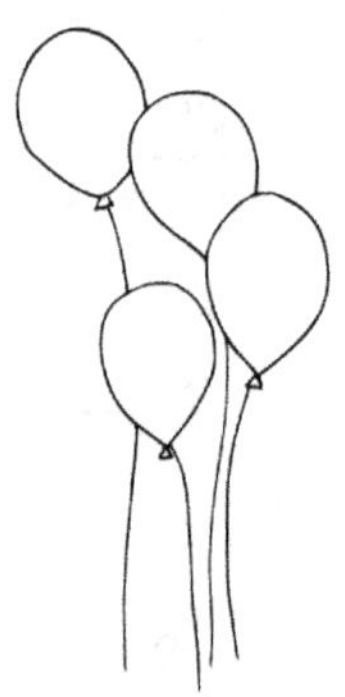

MAY BE

May be one day, I can touch a star,
Cradle it in my hands,
And share its shimmer with all I love.

May be one day, I can ride the wind,
Learn to travel with it,
And decipher the secret of the eye of a tornado.

May be one day, I can finally understand,
The meaning of this life,
And why I love what I love.

May be, just may be one day,
I can find out who I am.

CRAFTER'S WAY

Gently very gently,
She crafted her pieces,
Deliberately she drew the strokes,
Softly contouring the curves and figures.

Each piece was contrived,
With focus and with prayer,
Pondering on the beauty,
Immersed in the creation.

Lost to the world,
Lost in the moment,
She brought to life,
A miracle out of void.

TRANSIENCE

Each moment slips away unnoticeably,
Without any clamour or alarm,
Each second melts smoothly to the next,
Unaware of its transience, we let it flow away,
The feel of my baby's hands in mine,
The sweaty smell of his unwashed hair,
The way he celebrates each day,
So much has already gone,
I try to hold on tightly and preserve each
moment,
But years later my memory may not hold all the
colours,
I dread the day I may forget the warm hugs and
kisses,
The first day of his school and the day he started
reading,
The moment his little fingers finally maneuvered
a button into its hole,
The day he had a meal on his own,

His first drama and storytelling,
Precious moments to be cherished forever,
But these moments are treasures only for me,
And when I pass away, it will be erased from
this world forever.

DOSE OF LOVE, HOPE AND COURAGE

After all the world is sweet,
With a topping of rainbow sprinkles,
Hug from loved ones,
Sweet innocent smiles,
And utter faith in our love.

After all life is worth living,
With a dash of imagination,
A sprinkle of fairy dust,
A dose of love, hope and courage,
And a pinch of stories of unknown lands.

MAKE A CHANGE

Is it possible to catch a rainbow in our hands?
Is it possible to snatch an Indian milkweed on its
flight?
Is it plausible to dance with flowers?
Or drift with the clouds?
Is it feasible to contain a volcano?
Is it viable to merge with the ocean?
Is it imaginable to survive a tornado?
So why are we powerless humans,
Fighting amongst us and with nature?
Why do we spend our effort and energy,
To methodically destroy our home, earth?
Why do we demolish anything we cannot
create?
Instead let us spend our time building up a better
world,
Let us share our resources as nature teaches us,

Let us begin a different stream of thought for a better life.

HELLO SADNESS

Through tear-filled eyes,
I saw your face and thought you were strange,
And then I met you again,
I thought it curious that all our rendezvous were
accompanied by tears,
Yet through laughter-filled days,
I started missing you and longing for you,
Your absence left a hole in my heart,
And I sobbed and weeped without a reason,
All I could comprehend through the haze,
Was my desperation to meet you again,
I realized flabbergasted that I had fallen for our
tear-stained faces.

LIFE IS A LONG WAIT

We wait, wait and wait,
For good days to arrive,
And bad ones to be over,
We wait with anticipation for a break,
And then we wait for the next one,
We wait for the next big success,
And the next holiday to celebrate,
We wait for reasons to be happy,
And our sadness to pass away,
We wait for our children to mature,
And then realise with regret that the best days
have passed by,
We wait for love,
And then we wait for freedom,
We wait to rest and then we scamper in a hurry,
And so this cycle continues,
Till we leave for eternity.

CHANGE CHAMPIONS

She holds her baby close,
Her heart beating against it,
She is just a mother with her son,
As perceived by the common eye,
But beneath is hidden her story,
One unbeaten by struggle or pain,
One lone hero, trudging through life.

He cycles through the long winding road,
Withered and worn, he resembles an ordinary
man,
Peel through the layers of daily grind,
To discover the change champion of many lives.

See the dame with silver hair,

Gaunt like a reed,
She has raised many, fed many and strengthened
many.

They flow through life silently,
Helping and empowering,
Unsung they remain, unknown to the world,
Yet etched in the hearts of those they touch.

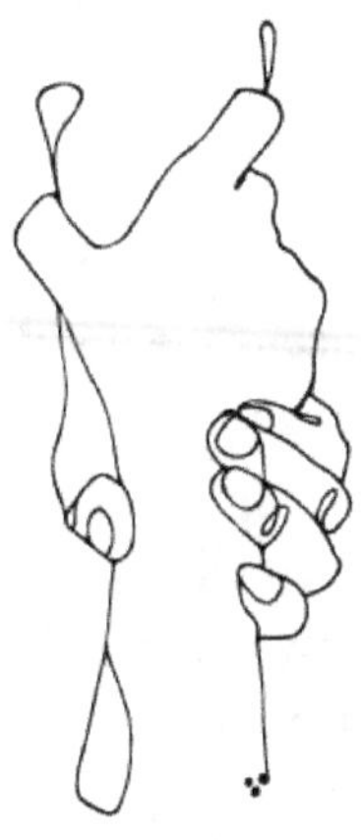

PEACE

Peace means a world of truth,
Where benevolence is the norm,
And every child is sheltered.

A world of courage and hope,
A world of sincerity and happiness,
A world of imagination and purity.

Peace is when we wake up with a smile,
Engage ourselves in higher pursuits,
And embody our deepest passions.

Peace is our ultimate state of existence,
The one we strive for,
The one we endeavour to merge eventually.

JOURNEY THROUGH LIFE

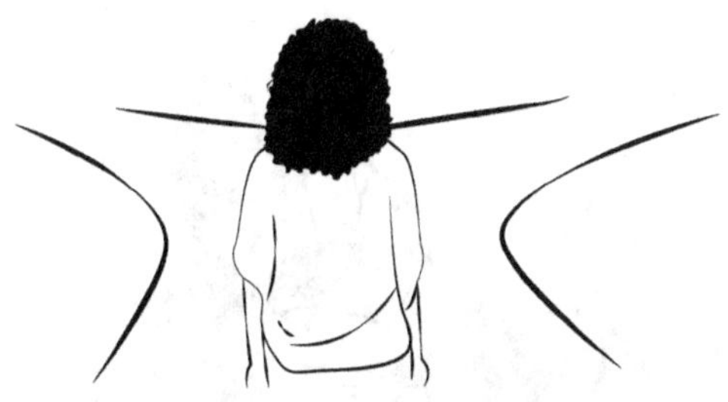

I wish for the night to stretch to eternity,
With dots of life streaming fast,
Both above and below, within and without,
As I travel with cities flying past,
I feel disembodied from life itself,
And all my past, present and future blur,
All the troubles disengage from me,
And the cords of attachment are severed,
If only the night never ends,
I will finally be free from the paraphernalia
needed for this existence,
From wishes, dreams and emotions,
From expectations, presumptions and duties,
If only this journey never ends,
I suppose I will discover my essence,
And who I am.

CONSTANT COMPANION

Have you watched the flickering shadows,
They cast such pleasing pictures everywhere,
Even on your face, which otherwise would be
just "another normal face",
But shadows add texture and depth,
Hollows and valleys, adding poetry,
Unknown to the bearer,
Beholden only by a fine artist,
They dance and hide,
At times they pop in tandem,
They give constant company in light,
And when darkness falls, they melt into you,
Staying within your heart,
Singing long forgotten haunting songs of the
deep,
They stay by your side until your last breath,

If only we could learn to hold their hands,
We wouldn't be so lonely in the multitude.

25

BRIGHTER WORLD

Let us unite to make this world a safe zone,
For our kids, our parents and ourselves,
Let us wake up each day with hope,
Let us create a world where kids live with
wonder,
Run around gleefully with their innocence intact,
And look up to us with a glint in their eyes,
Let them share and care without fear,
Climb trees and play around freely,
Under the loving eyes of grandparents, uncles
and aunts,
Let them be blissfully unaware of wars and
brokenness,
Of the deep dark abyss and threats,

Let them spread their wings and fly,
And when the time comes, let them unite their
strength for a brighter world.

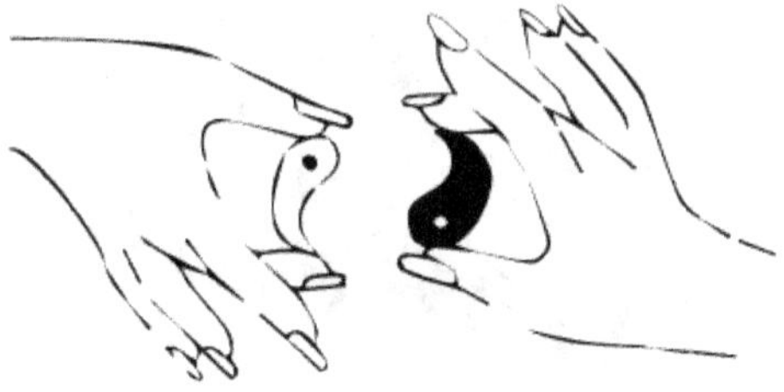

DEAR DIARY

As the last leaves of this year fall,
And the last pages are filled in,
I prepare myself to bid you farewell,
I am ready with a new one,
To pen my thoughts and emotions,
But for the first few months,
I will regret your loss,
I will surely yearn to write in you,
I will sorely miss the year that ran by in a flash,
The laughter and memories of the year gone by,
Leave a rivulet in my sad heart,
And I shall rest peacefully with the knowledge,
That they are indelibly recorded in my heart,
And on your pages,
To be revisited and reminisced with fondness,
In the coming days.

HOLD ON TO YOUR DREAMS

Hold on to your dream if you have one,
Let none discourage you from its pursuit,
Hold on, even if it seems impossible,
Toil more till the end is attained.

For your dream is your purpose,
No one else can feel it the way you do,
And if its grandeur frightens you,
Strive longer and harder till it is achieved.

No castle is built in a day,
So it is, with your aim,
Tackle it each day for a moment or more,
Strive till the end.

And when you are defeated and beaten down,
And the world stares smugly at you,
Rise up like a phoenix,
And try just one more time.

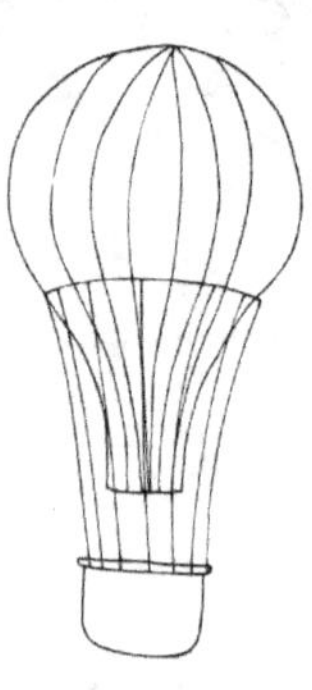

WINDOWLESS ROOM

I enslave my dreams,
To be seen and heard by none,
When the sun shines spreading glorious light,
My dreams wither and wilt away,
When the spring rain cools the earth,
And sparkling rainbow adorns the sky,
My colourless soul mourns in sorrow,
In a windowless room my soul slumbers,
Never to be awakened,
Never to be discovered.

ENJOYING THE MIDLINE

I walk on the dividing line,
Not here, nor there, I hang in midline,
I walk on the seashore,
One foot in water, the other on sand,
Suspended in time,
I stand in the shadows hidden,
But the silhouette is in the limelight,
Not here, nor there, I stand on the midline,
Midline is fun and joyous,
I get the best of both worlds suspended in the
middle,
And if I choose to fly, sky is closer from here,
An almighty jump is all that I need,
Exploring the middle is enjoying the grey's,
And sometimes grey's are prettier than stark
white or black.

DREAM CATCHER

I hang a dream catcher in my room,
With longing and fear and unfulfilled wishes,
Maybe it will help me seize my dream by its tail,
And bring it to fruition.

Heaps of broken dreams are stacked up in the
corners of my mind,
On good days I forget my hallucinations,
On bad days, they haunt me and tease me and
smash me to a zillion pieces.

Dream catcher, catch all the splintered fantasies
in your web,
Do not let it trickle down your feathers,

Unless it has a laughter echoing down its
passage,
Hold them tight and grind the splinters,
Scatter them to the ends of the earth,
Away from human hearts.

HAUNTING MELODY

I once heard a song,
Never heard again, ever again,
Soulful and ardent,
It pierced my bleeding heart,
I sought for it in vain,
Fervent to heed its lyrics,
For just one more passing moment,
To feel its tender notes,
Wash over the shores of my soul,
Praying to catch the haunting melody,
And freeze it in the depths of my frozen heart.

SHINE LIKE A STAR

See the stars sparkling their heart out,
They burn and splutter,
In the void called space.

See the stars creating supernovas,
They explode and burst,
Unaware of us humans.

See the stars being their best,
Creating and consuming energy,
Even when no one requires them to.

See the stars and be one too,
Change the world with your brilliance,
Create a revolution with your life.

BEAUTIFUL WORLD

What if the world talked in verses,
Poetry dripping from each mouth,
Beautiful play of words,
Making each day, a little less uncouth.

What if we could all create art,
Scintillating paintings everywhere,
Each street, each wall,
A template for vibrant work.

Wouldn't life be a little less dreary?
Wouldn't our hearts be more glad?
Or would we all learn to acclimatise?
Familiarised with beauty, would we renounce it
all?

TO CONFORM OR NOT

Staring eyes, they disturb,
"Why aren't you like us?"
They question,
"Why don't you conform?"
They question.

But maybe I don't bother,
I shrug and turn away,
They disturb, but don't deter,
I glide through life,
To my own tune.

REASON FOR LIVING

She was dying and needed a reason for living,
He was living and sought a reason for dying,
The two met like galaxies,
Exploding like a giant supernova,
Neither could convince the other,
Of the worthwhile's or why's,
They challenged their faith in humanity,
They tackled the myth of existence,
They hated love violently,
And swore never to love another,
At last she left for her forever abode,
Leaving him with the reason he sought.

STOP DEAR TIME

Time! I bid you to stop,
Stop when my child smiles,
And all his innocence be preserved,
For ages and ages till the end of time.

Time! I implore you to stop,
Gather my dreams in your palms,
And blow it out to eternity,
For my child to catch in his future.

Time! Stop, stop and stop,
Each time my child watches a rainbow,
And learn to dream and sing,
And paint his life with goodness.

Time be his friend, always forever.

DEAR NOVEMBER

May you be filled with promises of hope,
May you sparkle with brilliance of life,
May you learn patience and peace,
May all your ambitions be fulfilled,
May the anticipations and strife of former days
flourish,
May the brokenness be healed to create beautiful
patterns in gold,
May you be enough, always and in every way.

SAFE HARBOUR

Deep inside we are searching for a safe harbour,
That place where we are embraced and
applauded for who we are,
Our mistakes forgotten and victories
encouraged,
But our earth is too old and tired for such a safe
haven,
A much-awaited resurgence is needed,
Both within and without,
To revitalize our soul and our home,
Let there be a fresh proposition,
A world of brilliance and kindness,
Generosity and compassion,
Let our children learn benevolence,
And humans learn to be humane.

DREAM OF A HERO

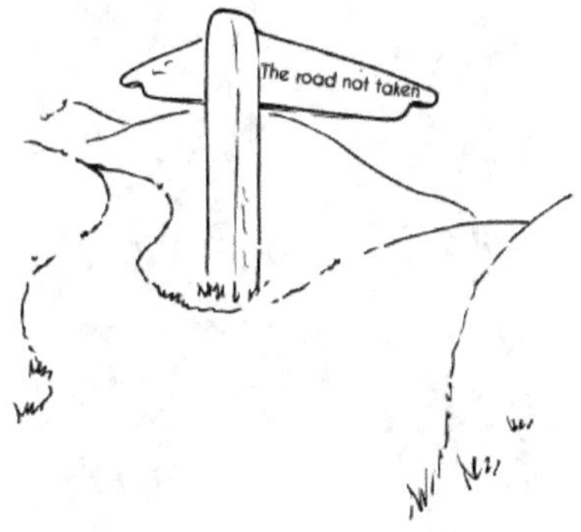

He had a dream,
To be strong and brave,
To be someone who inspires,
And light up others with a smile.

He had a dream,
To lend a helping hand,
To lift others up,
From despairs of hell.

He had a dream,
To be kind and caring,
To change the world for better,
He had a dream to be a Hero.

DEAR SOUL

I hope that one day you will realise,
That it is acceptable to ride the emotional
rollercoaster,
Happiness, sadness, anger or jealousy,
That a young soul matures and takes flight,
Growing through the myriad facets of feelings,
Finally embracing its oneness and its autonomy,
That a day will dawn with the epiphany,
That you are one with peace,
That everything else falls away like autumn
leaves,

Yet your essence will survive,
Having grown through the lessons of Life.

45

INDIAN SUMMER

The sun is unforgiving,
And rivulets of sweat run down the face and
spine,
The air is so humid and feels like it can be cut
with a knife,
The atmosphere is shivering with the heat,
The Indian summer is one, that has to be
experienced to be understood,
Children run around, untethered by heat,
While the elders languish in the prison of fire,
Trying to quench it by whipping up some cool
air or gulping down cool drinks.
The summer is relentless,
Even a short night shower leaves no trace by
morning,
Icecreams and soft drinks make a comeback,
And kids enjoy it all with glee,
While the elders perspire and fret,
Weighed down by the heat and their body.

A WISH FOR THE WORLD

With scrunched up eyes,
I hope on a shooting star,
To one day gather fairy dust in my hands,
I imagine it falling from my palms,
Spreading love and magic in its wake,
Softly I rub my hands together,
And it is palpable, so tangible,
I can almost feel its grains,
I see it covering the world in golden light,
Creating a shield of peace and goodwill around
us,
Let this goodness be unleashed,
Heralding good news and healing,
Transforming all darkness to light.